In Went Goldilocks

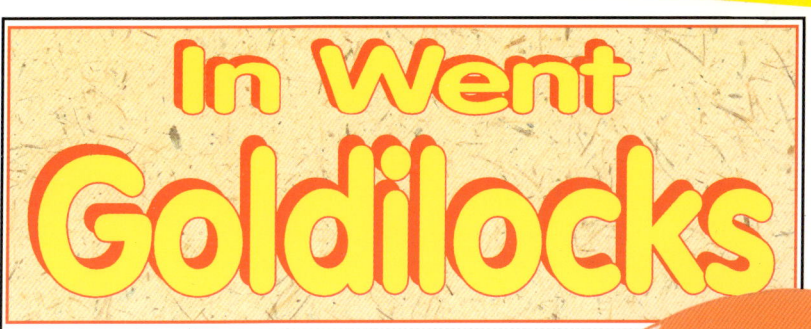

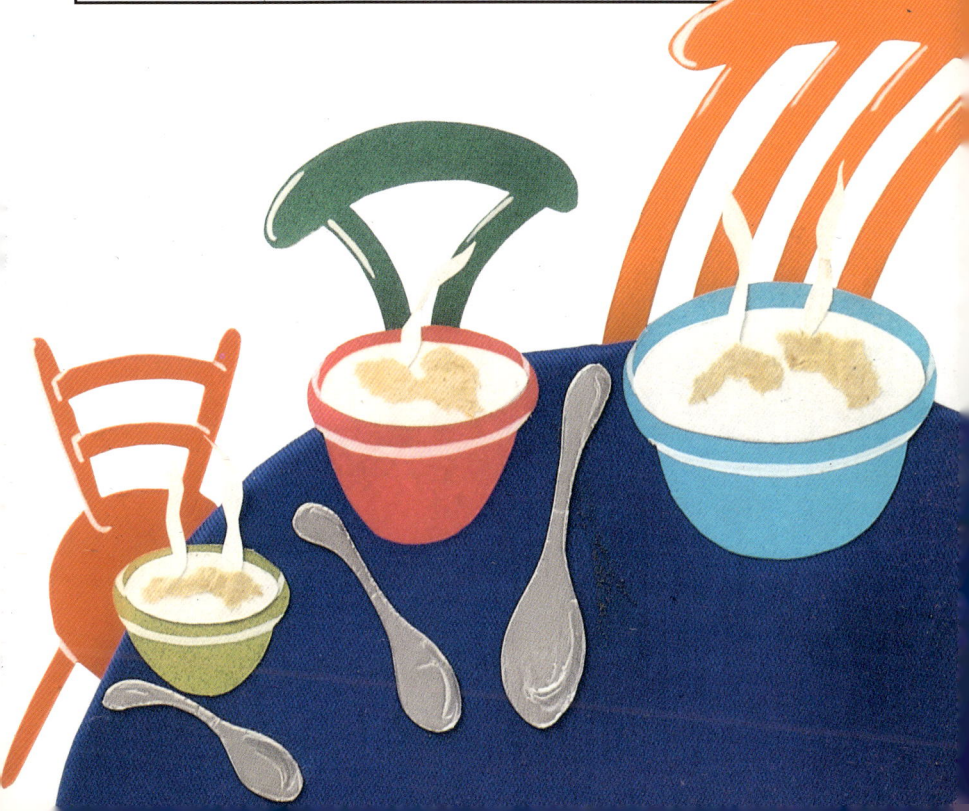

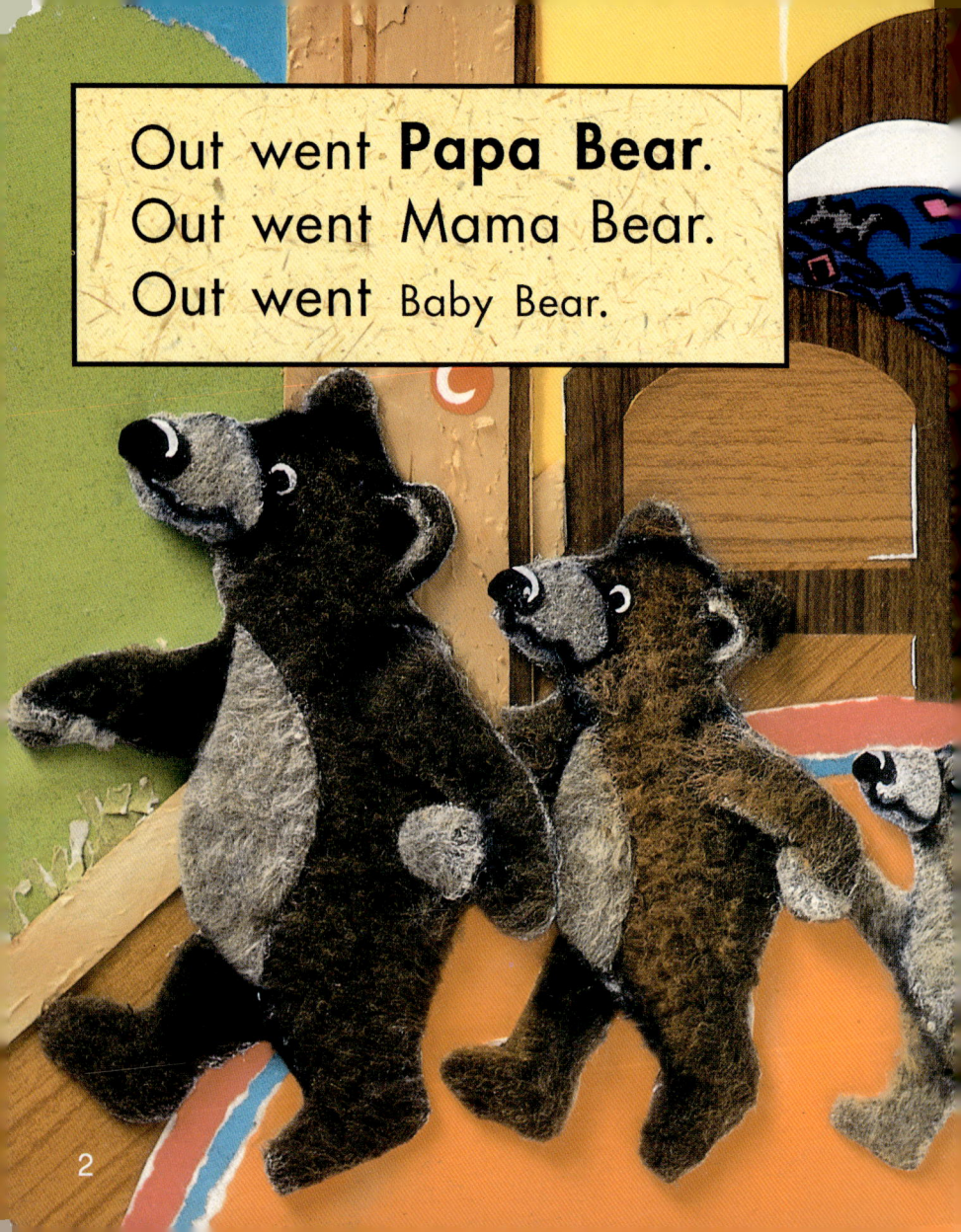

Out went **Papa Bear**.
Out went Mama Bear.
Out went Baby Bear.

3

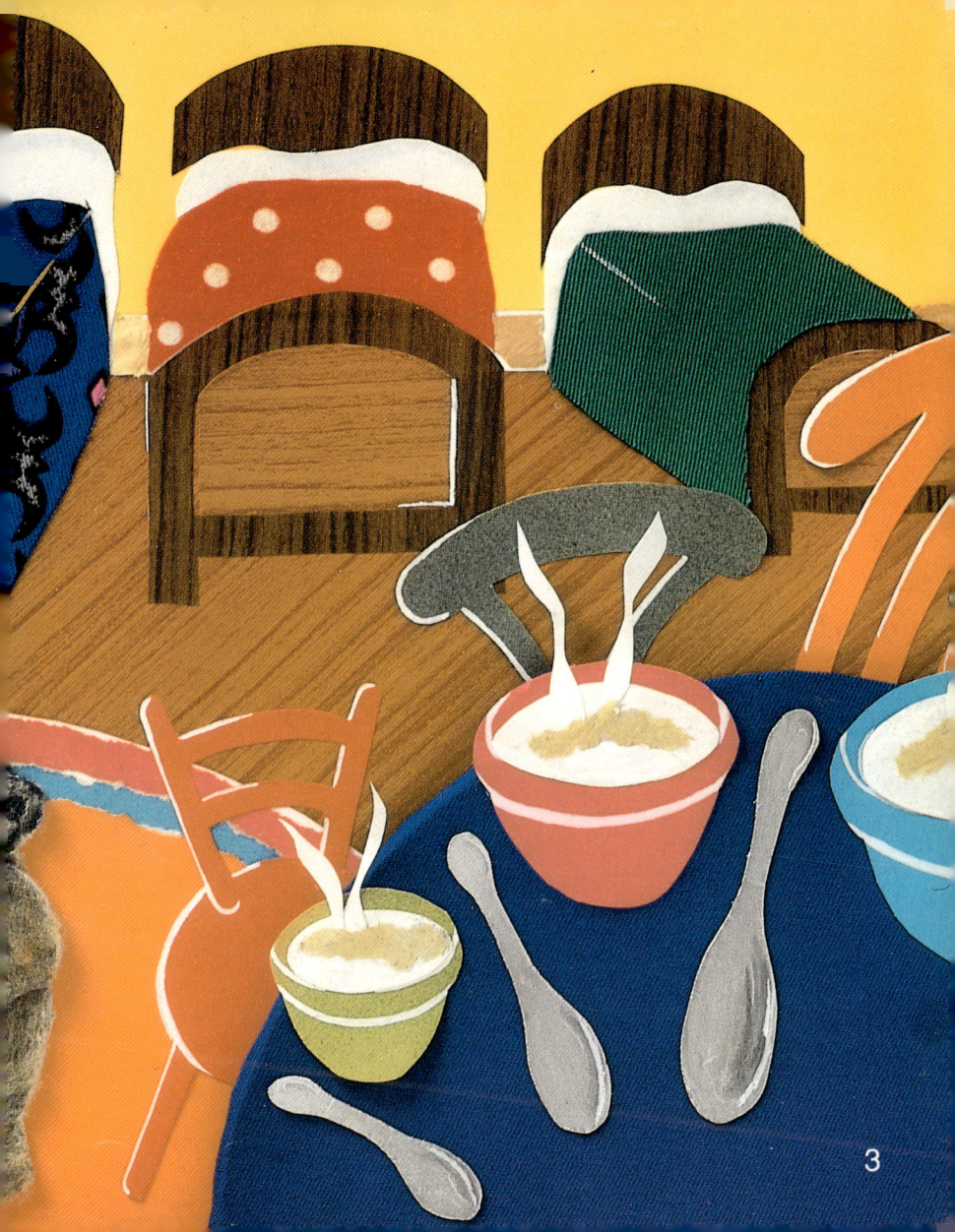

In went Goldilocks!

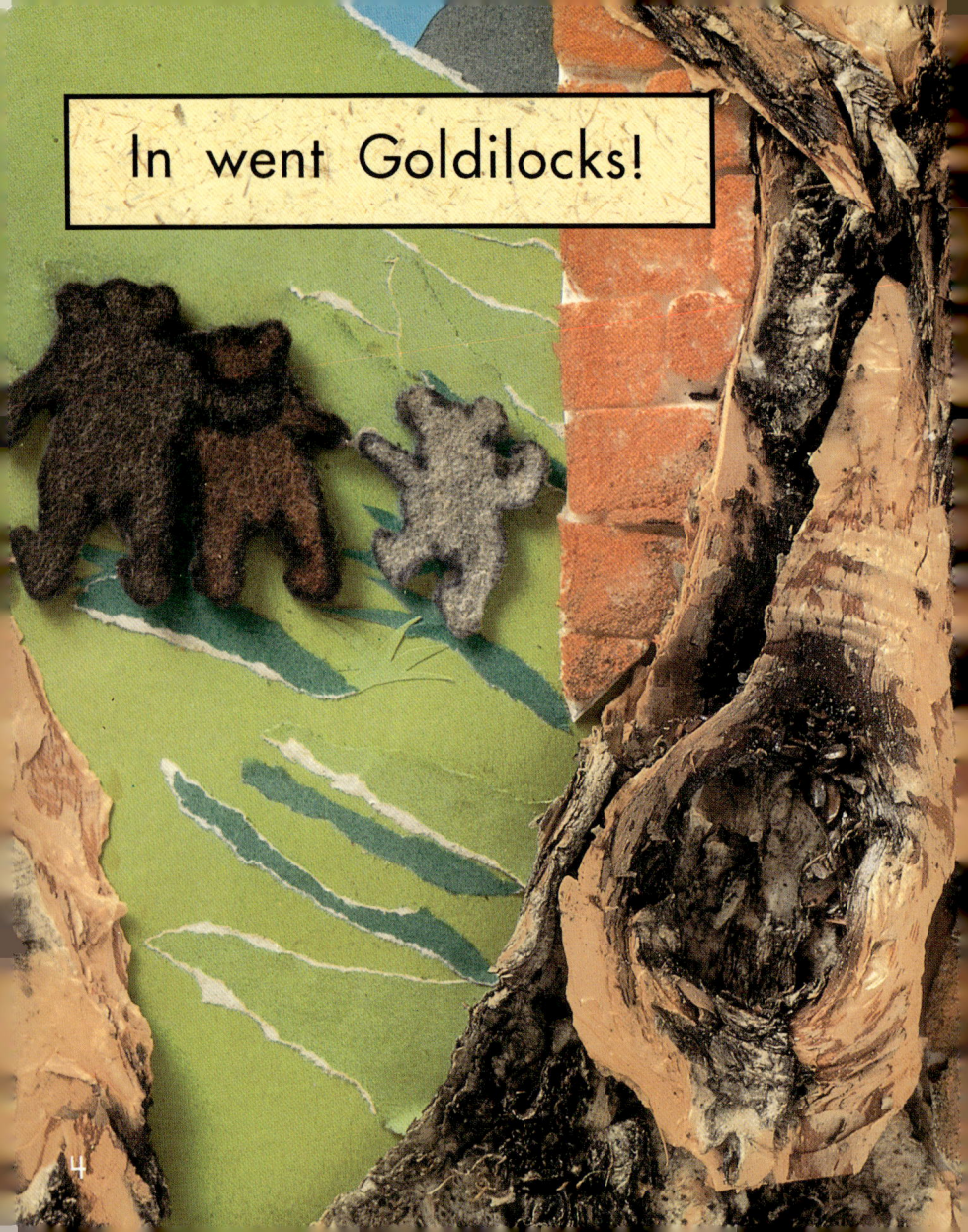

5

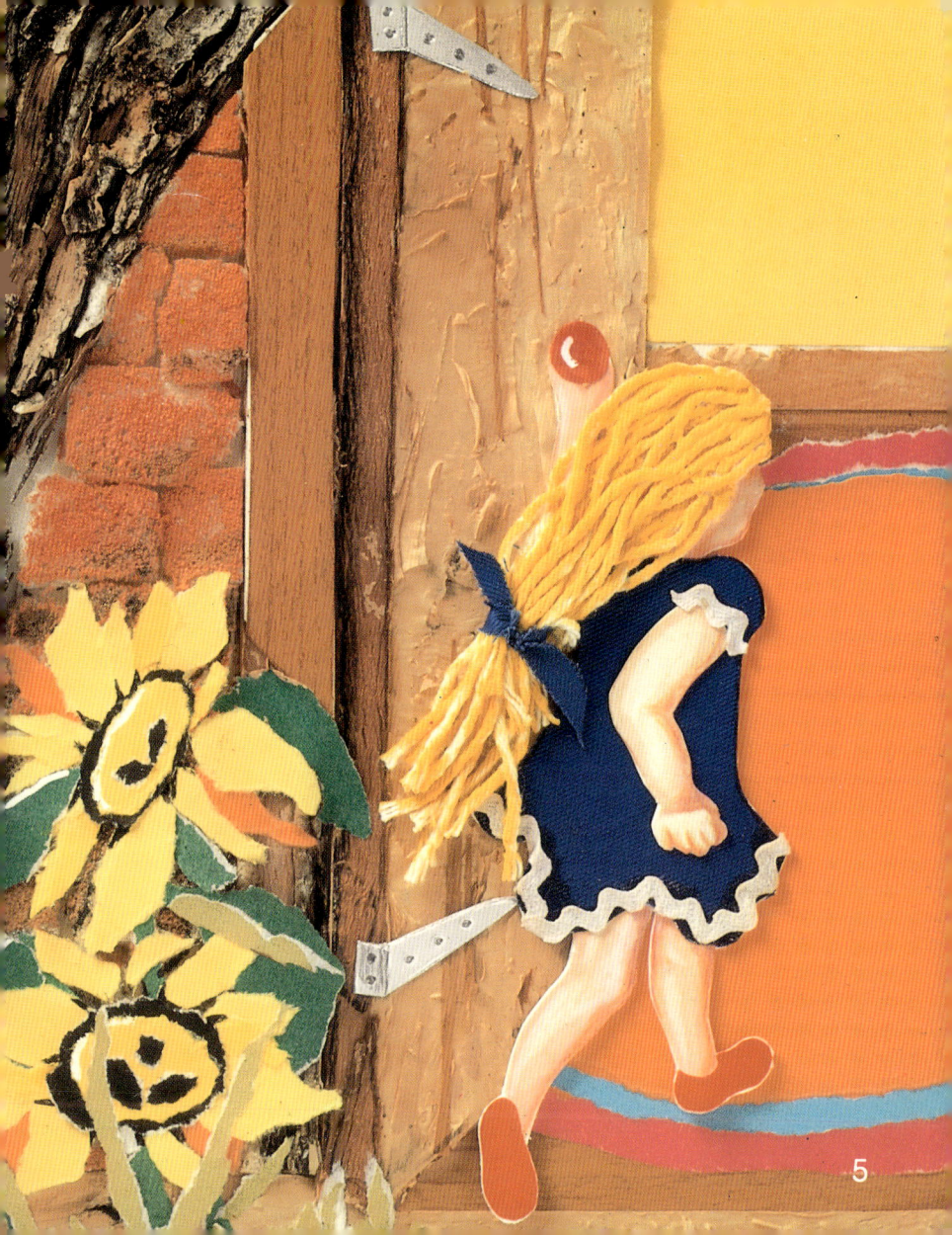

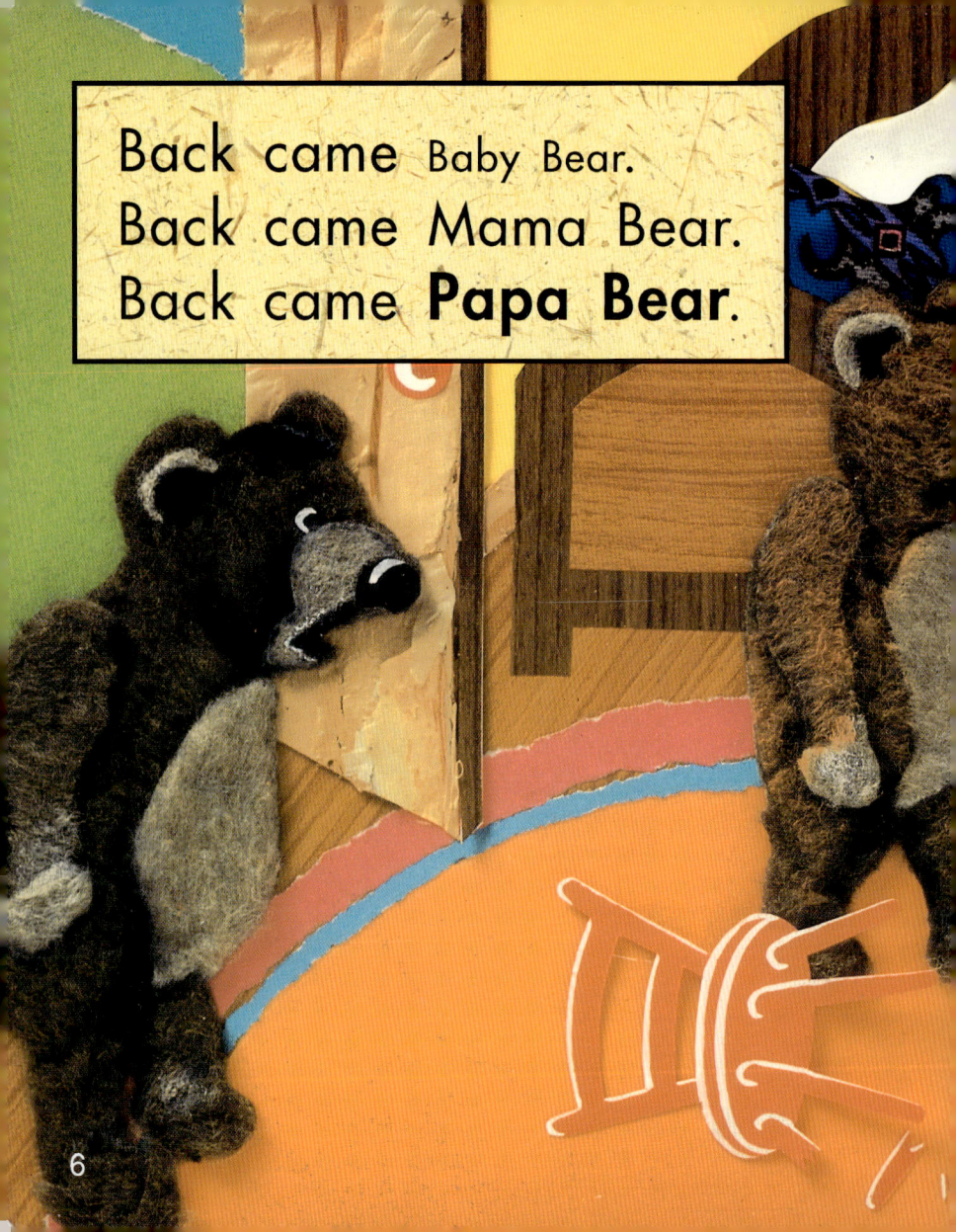

Back came Baby Bear.
Back came Mama Bear.
Back came **Papa Bear**.

7

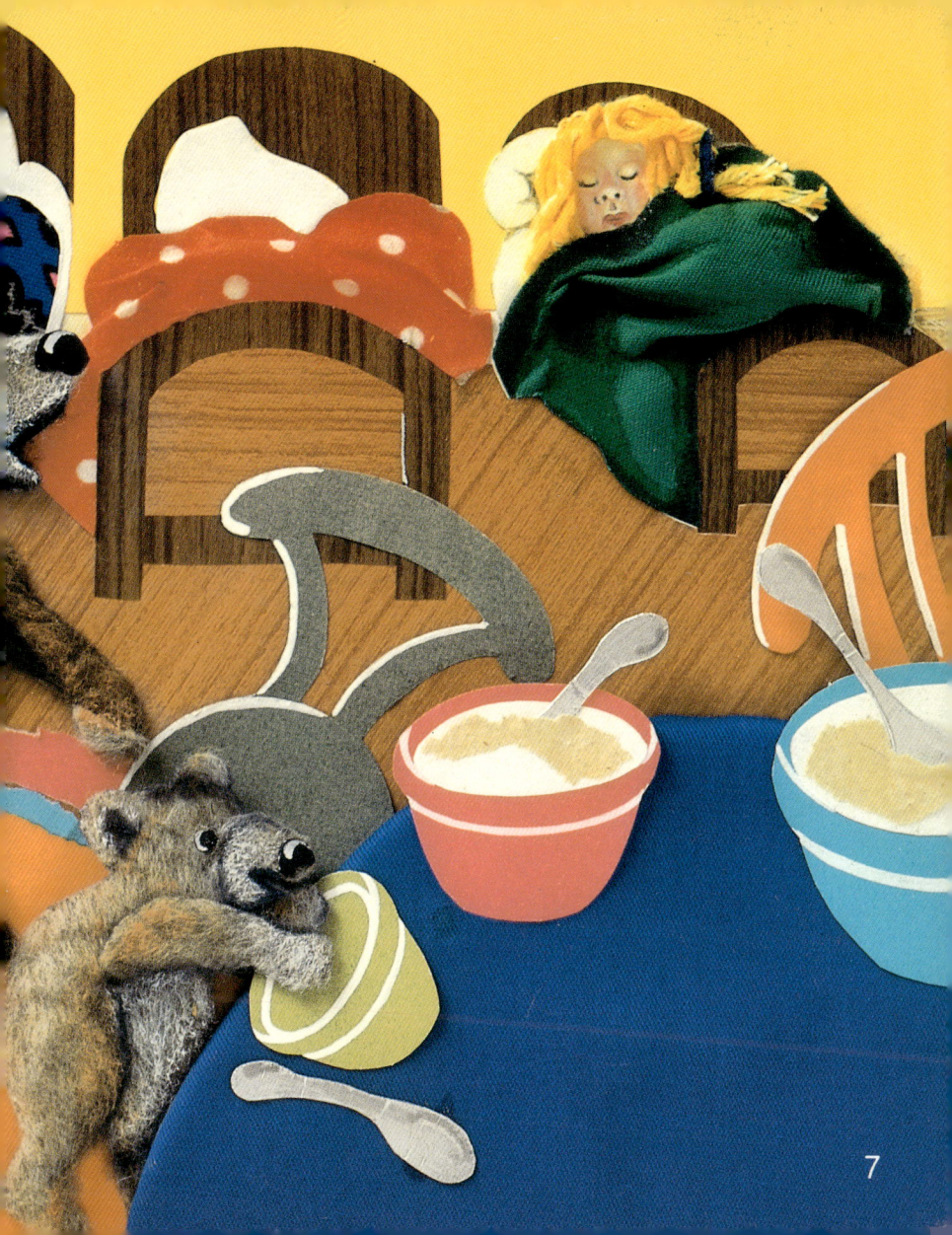

Out went Goldilocks!

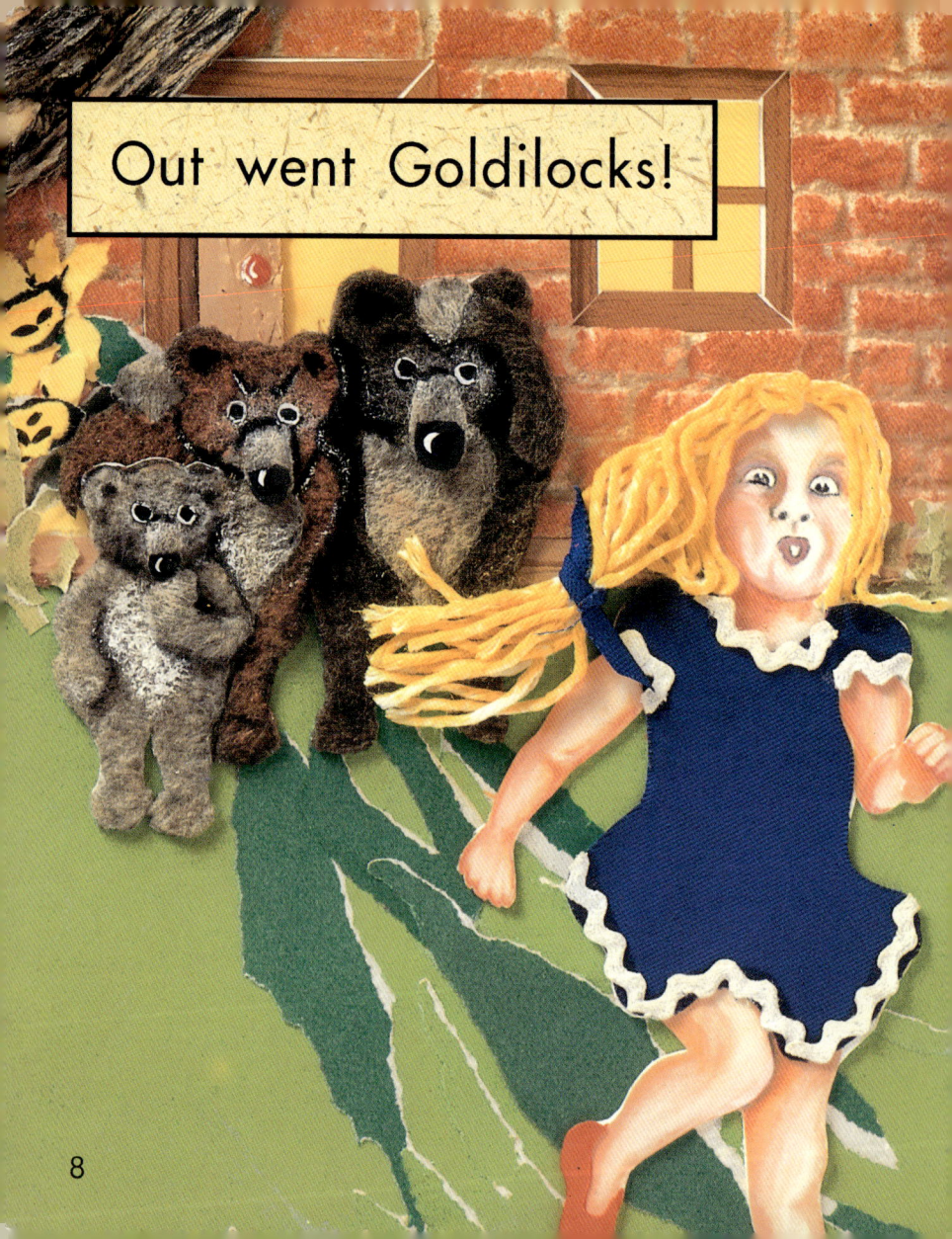

8